THE
DUFFER'S
GUIDE TO
SQUASH

Mike Gordon

COLUMBUS BOOKS LONDON

Other books in the Duffer's series:

The Duffer's Guide to Golf: A Second Slice (Gren)
The Duffer's Guide to Rugby (Gren)
The Duffer's Guide to Coarse Fishing (Mike Gordon)
The Duffer's Guide to Cricket (Gren)
The Duffer's Guide to Booze (Gren)
The Duffer's Guide to Rugby: Yet Another Try (Gren)
The Duffer's Guide to Snooker (Mike Gordon)
The Duffer's Guide to D-I-Y (Mike Gordon)
The Duffer's Guide to Getting Married (Gren)
The Duffer's Guide to Skiing (John Fairbanks)
The Duffer's Guide to Football (Gren)
The Duffer's Guide to Horse-racing (Mike Gordon)
The Duffer's Guide to Staying Married (Gren)
The Duffer's Guide to Electioneering (Gren)
The Duffer's Guide to Horse-riding (Gren)

Copyright © 1987 Mike Gordon

First published in Great Britain in 1987 by
Columbus Books Limited
19-23 Ludgate Hill, London EC4M 7PD
Reprinted 1988

Typeset by Cylinder Typesetting Limited,
48 Britton Street, London EC1M 5NA

Printed and bound in Great Britain by
Redwood Burn Limited, Trowbridge, Wiltshire

ISBN 0 86287 370 3

Author's note

*Many thanks to my wife Maria, and to Mr Bryan Parker and Mr Jonathan
Wylder for their time and generous assistance.*

CONTENTS

Foreword: 4

Squash – the Game: 5

The Court: 6

The Equipment: 8
1. The racket
2. The ball

Dressing the Part: 10

Types of Squash Club: 12
1. The run-down club
2. The city club
3. The smart suburban club
4. The multi-purpose sports centre

Squash Club People: 18
1. The manager
2. The coach
3. The receptionist
4. The men's captain
5. The ladies' captain

Types of Squash Player: 24
1. The designer-label player
2. The dangerous player
3. The bright and early player
4. The serious player
5. The sexy lady player
6. The natural
7. The 'take-it-easy' player

How to Improve Your Game: 32
1. Calling the score
2. Running
3. The video
4. Morris dancing
5. The ball-feeding machine
6. Teach-yourself books
7. The optical aid

I Play Squash Because . . . : 40

Are You League Material?: 50

Tactics (how to psych out your opponent): 59

Shots and Strokes: 68
1. The overhead volley
2. The miss
3. The disguised shot
4. The drop shot
5. The boast
6. The bullet shot

Squash Talk: 75

Foreword

Every day, millions of people lock themselves within four walls and test their skill, their speed and power and their ability to dodge little rubber balls.

These are squash players. For most the racket swings and the ball bounces. For others the racket bounces and the ball swings. This guide is dedicated to the latter contingent.

Squash – the Game

Squash is usually played by two players taking it in turns to hit, with a racket, a small ball against a wall. However, there are some variations: hitting the racket against the wall while dodging the ball, or hitting your opponent with the racket before he can hit the ball.

The idea is to develop your game until you find a strategy which affords you some fun yet ensures you still come out alive.

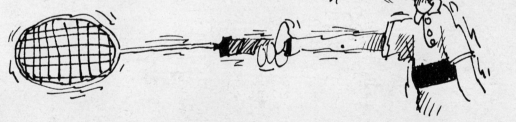

The Squash Court

1. The 'T' – best area to play from.
2. Short line – always worn away in the middle and blurred by 3.
3. Bloodstains – from players fighting for position on the 'T'.
4. Board – line to show area below is 'out'.
5. Tin – noisy metal sheet to make it really embarrassing when the ball is 'out'.
6. Spare kit – tactically positioned to soften impact of players and balls with tin.
7. Service box – to look foolish in.
8. Lights – source of balls in club shop.
9. Walls – designed for balls to bounce off, not players.
10. Cracks – resulting from impact of players with walls.

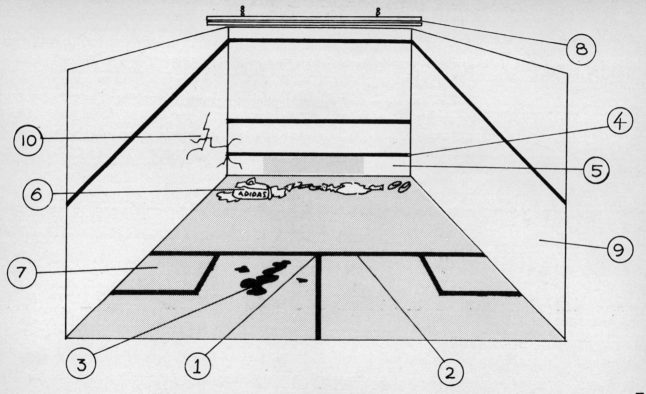

The Equipment

Any player with a pair of knobbly knees and hairy legs whiter than his shorts probably feels a fool. All he needs are the following two essential pieces of equipment – then he can act like one, too.

1. The racket

In the right hands the racket becomes more of a thin, fast-moving, hard-edged club.

As a duffer, however, you should start with a nice second-hand model with a really scruffy towel-wrapped handle, a few nicks and a couple of missing strings.. This will give you an awe-inspiring, battle-scarred air that could provide you with an *edge*, but at the very least will be a great excuse for your poor performance on court.

2. The ball

This soft, rubbery, round object gives squash its name. And so it should – because 'squash' is what it does to any soft bits like eyes, noses, etc. that might wander innocently across its path. This little missile also comes colour-coded with a small dot, so you can choose the one you think is prettiest. However, you should always try to avoid both the following:

No dot   You've brought the dog's ball by mistake.

Black dot   This is really the hole where you fasten the elastic that should be tied to your racket.

9

Dressing the Part

As a squash player you should dress the part frequently, even when you're not about to play. You will immediately have the admiring gaze of the public, especially the opposite sex, and be deemed to possess such qualities as health, fitness and dedication. This can be very nice, particularly when you're just weaving your way back from a social evening at the Dog and Ferret.

The rig-out should comprise:
1. Wristband (stops too much blood rushing to the brain)
2. Complexion (only thing whiter than shirt)
3. Goggles (ready for sun-bed)
4. Sweatshirt (living up to its name)
5. Designer ketchup stain
6. Handicap weight (differs for each player)
7. Alternative strip (for weedy players of either sex)
8. Extra balls
9. Headband
10. Towel
11. Spare handles (to look like extra rackets)
12. One and only racket
13. Other kind of squash
14. Trainers with white bottoms (to match yours)
15. Sports socks (lined with four pairs of odour-eaters)
16. Moustache (mark of a champion).

Types of Squash Club

Take some care over your choice of club. Although there are basically only four types, you don't want to find yourself reduced to a quivering mass of jelly five times a week when all you really want is a quick, ten-minute knockabout before you get back to the bar.

1. The run-down club

Half the membership here thinks it belongs to a tennis club. It used to have two squash courts until some of the drinking members shifted the billiards table into one.

When you check in, you get a broom to sweep up the plaster and a bucket for the drips from the squash-court roof. The holes in the ceiling are actually the main source of light, apart from the doorway. There is an old brick, though, if you prefer to keep the door closed. The duffer will enjoy the friendly atmosphere of a run-down club and should try to seek one out.

2. The city club

This club's full of trendy executives, especially at lunchtime. Everyone's playing for promotional stakes, trying hard not to beat the boss and making important deals in the sauna. If you've got a Filofax stuffed down your shorts or a telephone pager that bleeps all through the match, your prestige rating will go way up.

Despite the very high membership fees you should join the city club, if only to get the swanky membership sticker.

3. The smart suburban club

Competition at this club starts with half the membership trying to book the sun-beds at the same time. In fact, you can spot veteran members by their all-year tans. Health and fitness are also vigorously pursued at this club — not only on the dozen top-quality courts, but also through personal torture at the gym and in the sauna.

The duffer should be warned and take out social membership only. The suburban club's fee is not quite as hefty as the city club's but the sticker is still very nice and much sought-after.

4. The multi-purpose sports centre

This is full of interesting features which the duffer will find a welcome distraction:

1. Viewing gallery
2. Bar
3. Gym with sun-bed
4. Revolving doors
5. Ladies' showers
6. Gents' showers
7. Squash court 1: also site of Ladies
8. Squash court 2: aerobics class, kamikaze karate class, Women's Guild polo team and David Dork's basket-weaving classes
9. Fire exit and back entrance
10. First aid cupboard
11. Five-a-side football court
12. Viewing window to ladies' changing room
13. Archery targets
14. Café
15. Front entrance
16. Club mascot
17. Entrance/exit for gents' showers.

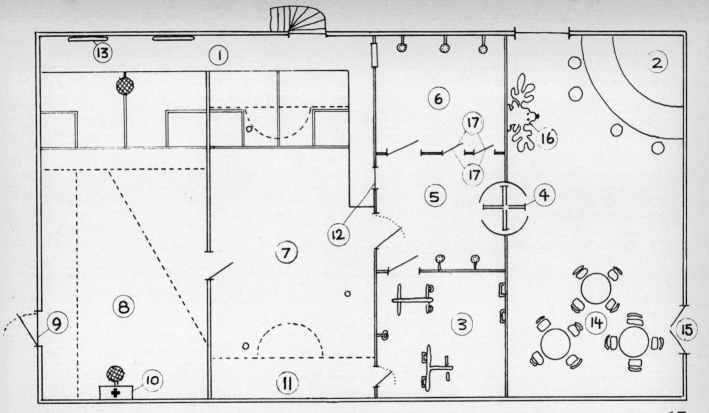

Squash Club People

There are certain key figures that the duffer will run into at almost every club. So that he can recognize them instantly when he meets them, the duffer should study the next few pages and learn which ones to blame for the rubbish hire rackets, weak beer, etc.

1. The manager

This bloke owns at least one of the Jaguars in the car park. This is because he makes hundreds of business contacts from those who take out a squash club membership as an essential business qualification.

Despite his hard nose for business, he usually looks pretty laid-back and tends to dress in track-suits. This is to catch you unawares as you undergo after-match resuscitation at the bar.

Before you can say 'no' to another gin and tonic, he's got you paid up for Life Membership, Superlife Plus and the Gold Racket Special Bonus Membership.

2. The coach

This member of staff can spot a duffer by the way he unzips his tracksuit. He's seen so many duffers he has a permanent air of resignation about him and a sigh that would make Lassie whimper.

He's often the local Mr Universe and when he's not coaching he's on the weights or spit-roasting in the solarium. Male duffers should book well ahead as the ladies usually get in first.

3. The receptionist

This deceptively mild-looking lady makes sure everyone knows the importance of her job. She does this by making you wait at least fifteen minutes before returning to the booking desk to check you in or answer the phone.

When you do get through to book, she will of course give you exactly the court time you want – over her dead body.

Nobody says too much because they all know she can thrash the pants off half the premier league and inform the manager of that little matter of your overdue subs at the spin of a racket.

21

4. The men's captain

The men's captain is most often seen hovering in the lounge, bribing and blackmailing other members to join the supporters on every away match of the season.

His tracksuit's covered in badges that make him look like at least a national player. On closer inspection these often turn out to be his son's scout badges.

A nice enough chap if you can stand listening to match statistics all day.

5. The ladies' captain

A formidable lady this, forever organizing matches, tea and sandwiches, the men's captain, the coach, the manager . . .

She'll make sure the club is represented at every possible venue. If she's a couple of players short, male duffers should beware. She'll grab a wig, stuffed bra and any passing male club member to take their place.

Types of Squash Player

Squash players are recklessly free with their telephone numbers. But don't expect ever to hear the husky tones of the dishy lady you spotted in the club lounge. True squash players have nothing but squash on their minds. Instead, learn to spot the following types – and never answer the phone in person.

1. The designer-label player

This type spends a lot of time showing off in the club lounge, positioned so that the light glints on his gold fillings and picks up the highlights in his hair. He's almost never seen without dark glasses, even on court, and his underpants are probably handmade in Italy by virgin seamstresses.

You can impress this sort by squeezing into your old school PE kit embroidered in some poofy colour with your initials.

25

2. The dangerous player

This type has just one blind spot – his opponent. He smashes around the court, completely oblivious that he's not the only person present, with the footwork of King Kong and a swing like Attila the Hun's. His is the most upwardly mobile name on the league ladder, leaving behind it a trail of broken noses and bruised ribs, property of those who got out of the way too late.

Avoid this sort unless you fancy a short stay in hospital.

3. The bright and early player

This player usually turns out to be the one you have to play to stay in the league. The only time he can fit you in – between coaching sessions, practice, more coaching, his high-powered job in the City, and yet more coaching – is at six in the morning. He'll ring you at 5.30 a.m. to confirm this.

While he's busy downing protein drinks and revving up his bio-rhythms, you'll be falling asleep in the showers.

Try intravenous coffee if you want to play this type.

4. The serious player

This player believes in the competitive spirit – he makes yours dwindle with his immaculate white kit and his six flashy rackets.

Once on court it's do or die, and by the second game it's usually you who's dying. Then, as you lie gibbering quietly on the squash-court floor, waiting for the stretcher, he'll kneel beside you in a truly concerned manner to ask, 'Er . . . Excuse me. That was my point, wasn't it?'

The duffer should do his best to become a serious player.

5. The sexy lady player

The sexy lady's game may not be well developed but everything else about her is. Matches against her are the closest squash comes to being a contact sport.

No healthy male stands a chance of returning her low-cut T-shirt combination shot. Male opponents also miss shots because they're busy admiring her tactical short-skirt play from the rear. Male duffers always emerge hot and flushed after a game against this type – but they're not usually too bothered about who won.

6. The natural

Until recently, this player thought squash was some sort of party game. He turns up in the remains of three rugby kits and disintegrating plimsolls looking like he just got out of bed.

Between yawns he goes on to play the meanest game of squash you've ever seen – with a tennis racket.

However, if you keep this amiable sort in the dark about the real rules for long enough you'll be able to explain that it was you who actually won.

7. The 'take-it-easy' player

This type limps on to court reeking of sprayed-on pain killer, hardly visible under elastic bandages, and asks if you'd mind taking it easy. Filled with sympathy and fellow feeling, but mainly with glee at the prospect of an easy win, you generously agree.

You start waving to spectators and trying out your Jonah Barrington impressions. Only when your opponent is about to clinch match point do you suddenly wake up and realize you've been conned. You should, of course, learn from this episode and try turning up in an ambulance for your next match.

How to Improve Your Game

No sensible duffer goes on lining the coach's pockets. Instead he should try improving his game, as outlined in the pages that follow. This is far less painful then paying someone to point out you're pretty hopeless anyway.

1. Calling the score

Fortunately, most duffers will rarely play in a match which requires a referee or a marker. This means you can volunteer to call the score. Do this precisely, carefully and accurately for the first game. After that, just as precisely and carefully, slip the odd point on to your score and the odd one off your opponent's.

Used properly, this method will enable you to make big improvements from match to match.

2. Running

Running develops speed and general fitness. There's no need, however, to go to the lengths of joining the running club. Instead, make it a much more rewarding experience by incorporating it into your everyday activities, so that rather than just running for its own sake you run to the pub, the Chinese take-away, the off-licence, the wine bar . . .

3. The video

This is a very popular stratagem of male duffers, who often get together for group analysis of their individual match performances on film. Or at least that's what they tell their wives.

4. Morris dancing

This is excellent for improving footwork. But then so is walking on hot coals.

5. The ball-feeding machine

Some duffers worry because they never see their squash balls eat anything at all. However, no duffers should really worry about the ball-feeding machine improving their game. Just for a change, here is an opportunity to win a few shots. With this in mind, there are only two settings you need to know:

Wrong   The balls look like this as they come at you like jet-powered hornets.

Right   The balls never come at you and you get a chance to whack the little buggers all over the place.

6. Teach-yourself books

These can be very handy so long as your opponent can be persuaded to read out the relevant instructions during the match.

7. The optical aid

This technique is used in the lounge. Simply stick a picture of a squash ball to the bottom of your glass. Such behavioural imprinting will greatly improve the way you keep your eye on the ball during matches.

I Play Squash Because . . .

As in any great sport, there's much more to squash than straightforward enjoyment of the game. Ask any seasoned club member. His answer, which will almost certainly be among the following examples, will reveal the complex psychological motivation of the squash devotee.

1. I like playing in the mixed league.

2. I like being close to my opponent.

3. You can never lose your balls playing squash.

4. I enjoy the changing-room heart-to-hearts.

5. I'm banned at the snooker club.

6. I love car stickers.

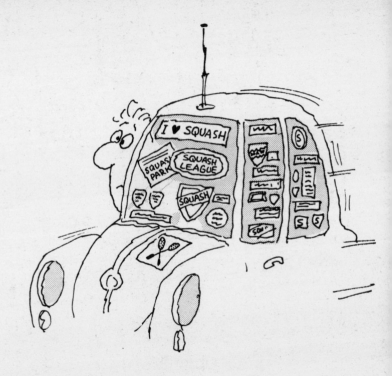

7. I get to thrash the living daylights out of my business rivals.

47

9. I can't stand the game, but I love all those girls in white.

Are You League Material?

Joining a league is as much a test of character as it is of your squash skills — which is a bit of luck really, so long as you can pass the following assessment.

1. Did you join your club because:

(a) The decor is lovely?

(b) The facilities are excellent?

(c) You like the view in the mixed sauna?

2. Do you want to join the league because:

(a) You believe in healthy competition?

(b) You know you can beat half the rest who have their names down?

(c) You've reformed since you were kicked out last time?

3. A visiting side narrowly beats your club's team. Do you:

(a) Buy the visitors a congratulatory drink?

(b) Buy the visitors a drink and tell your lot 'hard luck'?

(c) Let down the visiting side's tyres?

WHAT A LET-DOWN!

4. Reception has somehow double-booked your court. Do you:

(a) Call it bad luck and let the other pair play?

(b) Swear at the receptionist and split the time booked?

(c) Let the other pair take the court while you play with the receptionist?

5. Your opponent's shorts begin to rip. Do you:

(a) Cry 'let' and lend him a pair of your own?

(b) Hope it puts him off his game?

(c) Make him stretch for every shot to please the growing throng of spectators?

6. A game has been arranged with a member of the opposite sex. Do you:

(a) Refuse to play because of your unfair advantage?

(b) Refuse to play because you know you'll lose?

(c) Prance around like a lunatic trying to impress your opponent?

7. The running club captain suggests your game might improve if you join his outfit. Do you:

(a) Agree wholeheartedly and attend every session?

(b) Agree, but only turn up for their annual do?

(c) Disagree and explain that you already run with the crowd down at the Injured Sportsman?

8. You lost your last match because:

(a) Your opponent's play was far superior.

(b) You were suffering from a bad case of 'flu, but didn't like to say anything.

(c) Your opponent was a right pratt who always cheats.

Score 1 for each (a); 2 for each (b); 3 for each (c).

0–9   Maybe you should try ballet dancing.

10–17 Could do better.

17–24 Great stuff! It'll be your name on the cup.

Tactics

(how to psych out your opponent)

Some playing ability is nice to have, but it's not essential for the duffer. The following tried and tested methods will give your game a subtle edge by making your opponent's game as blunt as a door-knocker.

1. The tracksuit ploy

Never be the first to remove your tracksuit. Try and keep it on for the entire match. Your opponent will think you must be much fitter than he is. Of course, he shouldn't know you're *really* staying so cool because you've got nothing on underneath.

2. Tinned wins

Eat a large quantity of baked beans some time before a match. This ploy takes advantage of the confined space of a squash court.

WHAT HAPPENED TO THE THREE-MINUTE WARNING?

3. 'Chewing out' your opponent

Come on to court making a real meal out of a piece of chewing-gum. When it's your serve take it out and stick it in your ear. Once the serve's over, start chewing it again. This trick may taste terrible, but keep it up and by the last game your opponent should be feeling really sick.

The clincher on this one is to offer him the same chewing-gum before *his* serve.

4. The felt-tip ploy

This is a simple matter of colouring in the dots on the squash balls. The balls should always be your opponent's. That way you'll both keep quiet about the strange way all his fast balls seem to be playing a little slowly and he'll wonder if it's just him.

5. The 'protection' racket

On pretence of being a good sport, warn your opponent about possible imminent damage to his racket. Do this by shouting 'Watch your racket!' every time he starts his swing closer than five feet from any wall.

This works especially well with the serious player who probably had to take out a second mortgage in order to purchase his latest racket.

6. The legendary equipment ploy

In pre-match conversation with your opponent, feign great pride in your equipment. Humbly admit that the carbon fibre in your racket was actually extracted from Jonah Barrington's shin bone at great expense.

If he believes this, he's a right wally, and you can thrash him easily as he floats about in admiring awe.

If he doesn't believe a word, he'll think you're potty, drop his guard — and you can step in with a couple of blinders before he tightens up his game.

7. Bring the family

An assortment of relatives – spouse, children, grandparents, aunties and uncles – ranged across the gallery will considerably enhance your chances of winning by helping your opponent to lose. Being used to their little ways you will hardly notice the odd minor disturbance overhead. Your opponent, however, doesn't stand a chance. If the gentle but persistent shower of crisps, peanuts and lemonade cans doesn't put him off his game, the endless squabbling and whining will. Extra pocket money will also help as an encouragement to the kids to snigger softly every time he fluffs a shot.

8. The 'quick break' ploy

Use this routine when you're two down in a 'best of five', but never more than twice in the same game.

Feign an urgent need for a break. Go out, get your tracksuit back on, catch your breath, have a drink, a quick sauna and take in a couple of chapters of *War and Peace*.

When you return, pleasantly refreshed, apologetically mumble something about chicken tandoori, and then take full advantage of your opponent's state of cold, stiff numbness, developed during your absence.

Shots and Strokes

In squash, the main thing for duffers is to avoid playing the type of shot which could give you a stroke. Instead, concentrate on the type of shot which could give your opponent a stroke. The following examples show what we mean.

1. The overhead volley

This is a useful shot for returning nasty lobs. The object is to hit the ball as hard as possible at a very steep downward angle to maximize its rate of speed. It's called the 'overhead' because you do this directly over your opponent's head. Played correctly, it doesn't matter if it hits the front wall or not, as your opponent will be too concerned about his singed scalp to notice.

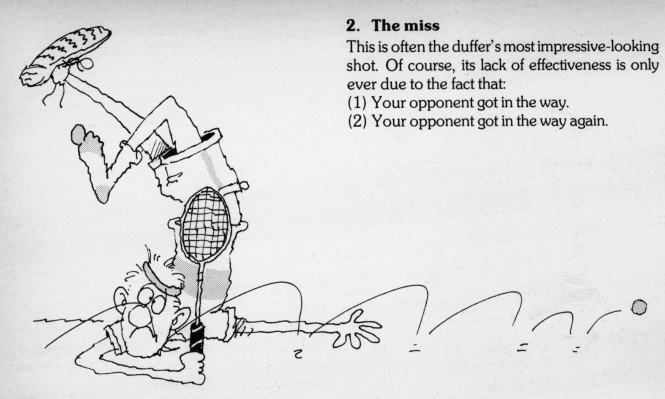

2. The miss

This is often the duffer's most impressive-looking shot. Of course, its lack of *effectiveness* is only ever due to the fact that:

(1) Your opponent got in the way.

(2) Your opponent got in the way again.

3. The disguised shot

At a push this can be another name for 'the miss'. Usually, it is any unintended stroke such as a lob that turns into a drop shot. When the disguised shot is a winner, never let on that you're as surprised as your opponent.

4. The drop shot

To the serious player this is the sneaky shot that caused the ball to bounce off softly into a front corner when you were waiting in a back corner to return it. The duffer, however, is much more likely to simply drop his shots than to play a drop shot – as when a speeding ball knocks the racket from his hand or his teeth from his mouth.

5. The boast

This is the shot played when the ball is coming at you so hard you've already turned and started running away. The ball just happens to bounce off your racket and is deflected off any old wall to score a winner.

When this does come off you should always brag about it – which is why it's called the 'boast'.

6. The bullet shot

This is the shot, played by your opponent, where you feel the ball before you see it. After intercepting the 160-mph paths of a few of these, you begin to feel like a homing beacon for a rocket.

Never attempt to return fire — no duffer's aim is good enough and anyway an 'accidental' neck chop from your backswing is a lot more satisfying.

Squash Talk

The duffer soon learns that a game isn't truly over until it's been analysed back in the changing rooms. This is where players compare excuses for bad shots and see who can exaggerate their best ones the most.

To join in, you too should learn the real meaning of intelligent-sounding comments such as the following.

I was experimenting with an unorthodox grip.
I tried to strangle my opponent.

The ball came off the side wall and up into my shorts.

My footwork wasn't up to scratch.
My shoelaces kept coming undone.

76

That rally in our third game was the best.
I won the point.

I was a bit heavy with the slice on my forehand volley.
I kept hitting the ceiling.

I think I sprained something early on.
My opponent won.

77

I'd anticipated the angle but the ball died in the nick.
The ball fell in the corner and I couldn't get to it.

My attack wasn't on form.
I kept missing my opponent.

I played a brilliant defensive boast.
I got lucky.

78

I think my follow-through needs some work.

I hit my nose as well as the ball.

My positional play was a little weak.
Most of the time I was in the wrong place.

Given another two games I'd have caught him easily.

In about two years I might be as good as my opponent.

I overhit that last length.
I smashed the gallery window.

**I don't know which is best—
my forehand or my
backhand.**
I don't know my left from my
right.

**I didn't know whether to use a lob or a
cross-court volley.**
I'd been picking my nose and wasn't looking.